Destiny's 1st Year Experience

with D.R.E.A.M
by Antionette Richardson

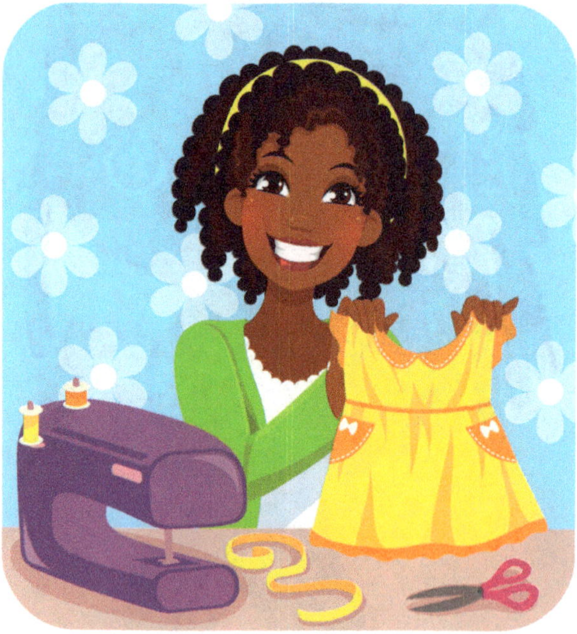

Destiny has such a collection of clothes to choose from!

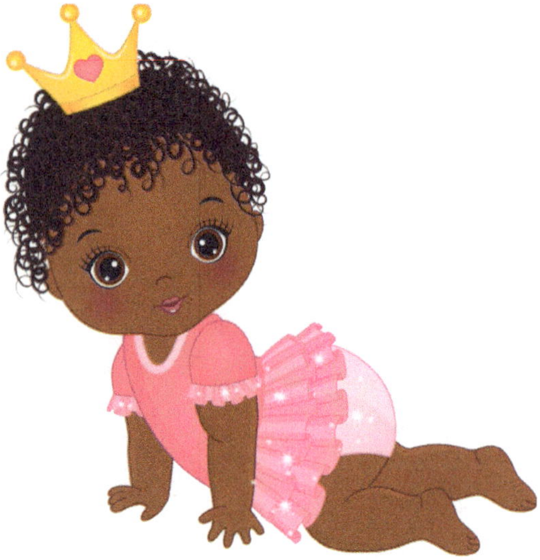

I am a beautiful Princess!

Destiny is so happy!

Shhhhh baby Destiny is sleeping
I am happy when I'm sleeping in my favorite color … purple.

Look at me!

Look at me, I am Destiny, What's your name?

Destiny takes a nap, she is very tired.

Ha ha ha look at those eyes on those fruits, criss-cross

Look at all of those healthy vegetables, we have green, purple and orange. Which one is your favorite of them all?

Destiny we will put your bottle away!

I love my eggplant

Hurry up, here comes time!

Destiny, let's count the wings on Miss Bumble Bee?

Look at how Milky is looking at me

Puff Bear is my name

Chapter 2

From Crib to School.

Time to rise and shine.

Destiny!

Destiny is so excited to get up.

Rub a dub dub it's time for the bear to scrub.

Can I have my breakfast now!

Destiny, we are going from the crib to school.

NOOOO BOTTLES!

WHAT IS FOR BREAKFAST?

What's for breakfast?

Always be PROUD of who you are.

FRUITS DOES THE BODY GOOD.
Apple a day keeps the Doctor away.

Friends, can you count the fruits?

Destiny and friends can you name the fruits with me?

Everyone is so happy!

Destiny and friends can you name the fruits?

BYE BYE FRUITS,
BYE BYE,
WE WILL SEE YOU
AGAIN NEXT TIME, BYE

Chapter 3

DESTINY GOES TO SCHOOL.
Hello, I'm here to take you to School.

Oh Destiny it's time for school!

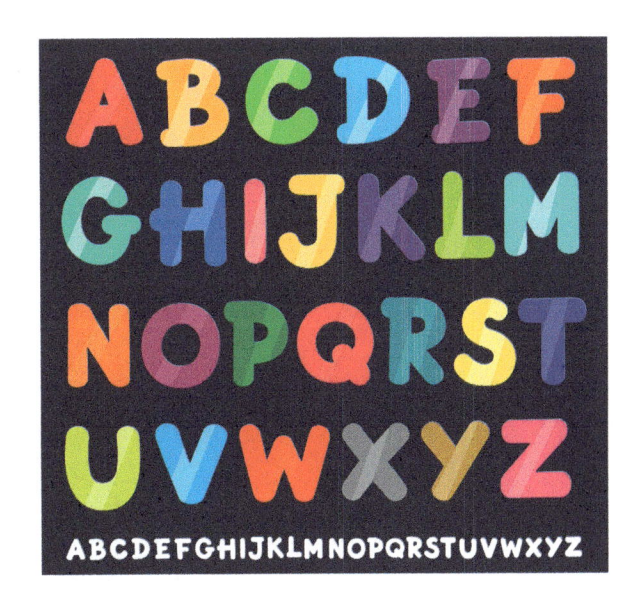

Take a look at the black board

WE ARE GOING TO ENGAGE IN ACTIVITIES.

CIRCLE	SQUARE	TRIANGLE
RECTANGLE	PENTAGON	DIAMOND
HEXAGON	TRAPEZIUM	STAR

WOULD LIKE TO INTRODUCE YOU TO MS. BEE

Buzz Buzz Buzz goes my wings.

Lady Bumble Bee said, "It's nice to be KIND."

"It's nice to be BRAVE."

Lady Bumble Bee said It's nice to be HUMBLE.

LEARNING NEW THINGS IS GOOD.
Lady Bumble Bee said, "It's nice to be CREATIVE."

I'M A HAPPY BEE.
Lady Bumble Bee said, "It's nice to be HAPPY."

CHILDREN YOU HAVE DONE A WONDERFUL JOB WITH YOUR SHAPES.

CIRCLE	SQUARE	TRIANGLE
RECTANGLE	PENTAGON	DIAMOND
HEXAGON	TRAPEZIUM	STAR

Destiny, can you tell me the color you are wearing?

I AM WEARING RED, BLACK AND WHITE COLORS.

I love Colors

Destiny loves to color

YELLOW	ORANGE	RED	PURPLE
BLUE	GREEN	PINK	GREY
GRAY	BROWN	WHITE	BLACK

What's Your Favorite Color?

Chapter 3

Sports Time!

Destiny loves to play golf.

Volleyball is my favorite sport!

Destiny is very athletic!

We love the outdoors!

Friends, it's time to go to the playground!

WE MUST WASH OUR HANDS.

Wash Wash Wash your hands. Wash them nice and clean.

Scrub Scrub Scrub your hands. Scrub them nice and clean.

Scrub Scrub Scrub your hands. Scrub them nice and clean.

Rinse Rinse Rinse your hands. Rinse them nice and clean.

Rinse Rinse Rinse your hands. Rinse them nice and clean.

Okay kiddies go and grab your lunch!

COMPARE AND CONTRAST THE FRUITS

CAN YOU NAME THESE FRUITS?

CAN YOU NAME THE YELLOW FRUITS?

CAN YOU NAME THE GREEN FRUIT?

CAN YOU NAME ALL OF THE ORANGE FRUITS?

MANY FRUITS ARE THERE?

WE HAVE A SPECIAL COLOR, CAN YOU NAME IT ?

OKAY CLASS CAN YOU TELL ME WHAT WE DO AFTER LUNCH?

1. Wash our hands.

2. Clean up.

3. Wipe the tables.

4. Wipe the chairs.

You did a wonderful job at cleaning up after yourselves

Chapter 4

NAP TIME

OH MY GOODNESS DESTINY! LOOK AT ALL THOSE PATTERNS AND COLORS.

OKAY FRIENDS REST TIME IS OVER! TIME TO PUT YOUR MATS AWAY.

I HOPE THAT EVERYONE IS WELL RESTED.

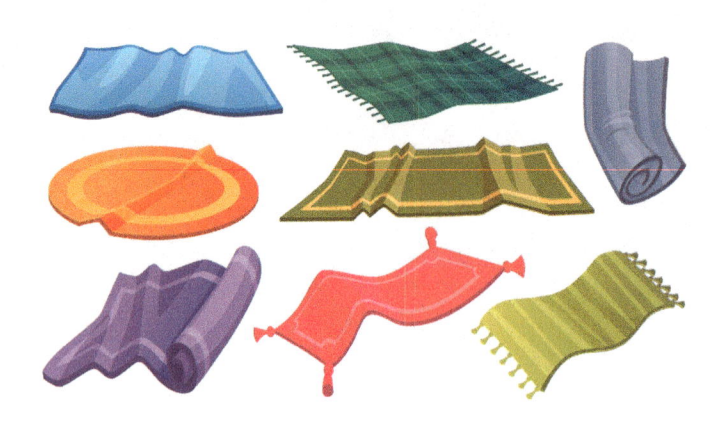

We are getting ready for our party.

DESTINY LOVES THE WATER

She dreams that one day she can swim with a dolphin as a mermaid.

You can use this to make a straight line. What is my name?

You may have to use this four times a day.

I am something that you write with. What is my name?

If you make a mistake, what am I?

Hip Hip Hur-ray I'm wearing my favorite color.

I can't wait to graduate!

How many books can you read?

We are ready for school!

D.R.E.A.M Dedicated to my grandchildren

Publishers: Andreanne Collections of Books & Princess Sarah MusicPublishing's (ASCAP) (Copyright@ 2015)
All rights reserved. No part of this publication May be
reproduced, distributed or transmitted Without the expressed consent of the Author.
All images and photos are subject to copyright, and owned by Fotosearch Inc and all
Artist within their Company ,
And all Artist permissions are only to be used by the Author of this work of Art

Made in the USA
Las Vegas, NV
25 October 2023